W9-AFE-748

NATURE'S GREAT JOURNEYS

SALMON

A JOURNEY HOME

M. J. COSSON
AND MARIA KORAN

MEDIA ENHANCED BOOKS
AV2
BY WEIGL™
ADDED VALUE • AUDIO VISUAL
www.av2books.com

AV² provides enriched content that supplements and complements this book. Weigl's AV² books strive to create inspired learning and engage young minds in a total learning experience.

Your AV² Media Enhanced books come alive with...

Audio
Listen to sections of the book read aloud.

Key Words
Study vocabulary, and complete a matching word activity.

Video
Watch informative video clips.

Quizzes
Test your knowledge.

Go to **www.av2books.com**, and enter this book's unique code.

BOOK CODE

J 9 9 6 8 4 5

Embedded Weblinks
Gain additional information for research.

Slide Show
View images and captions, and prepare a presentation.

AV² by Weigl brings you media enhanced books that support active learning.

Try This!
Complete activities and hands-on experiments.

... and much, much more!

Published by AV² by Weigl
350 5th Avenue, 59th Floor
New York, NY 10118
Website: www.av2books.com

Library of Congress Cataloging-in-Publication Data

Names: Cosson, M. J., and Koran, Maria.
Title: Salmon : a journey home / M.J. Cosson and Maria Koran.
Description: New York, NY : AV2 by Weigl, [2017] | Series: Nature's great journeys | Includes bibliographical references and index.
Identifiers: LCCN 2016004428 (print) | LCCN 2016007943 (ebook) | ISBN 9781489645234 (hard cover : alk. paper) | ISBN 9781489649959 (soft cover : alk. paper) | ISBN 9781489645241 (Multi-user ebk.)
Subjects: LCSH: Salmon--Migration--Juvenile literature. | Salmon--Juvenile literature. | Animal migration--Juvenile literature.
Classification: LCC QL638.S2 C683 2017 (print) | LCC QL638.S2 (ebook) | DDC 597.5/61568--dc23
LC record available at http://lccn.loc.gov/2016004428

Printed in the United States of America in Brainerd, Minnesota
1 2 3 4 5 6 7 8 9 0 20 19 18 17 16

072016
071416

Project Coordinator: Maria Koran   Art Director: Terry Paulhus

Every reasonable effort has been made to trace ownership and to obtain permission to reprint copyright material. The publishers would be pleased to have any errors or omissions brought to their attention so that they may be corrected in subsequent printings.

Weigl acknowledges Getty Images, Alamy, Minden, and Shutterstock as its primary image suppliers for this title.

Contents

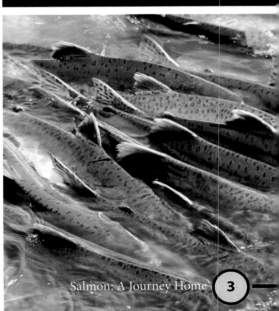

WILD SALMON

All wild salmon begin their lives in freshwater. They migrate to the ocean to live most of their lives. Then they return to freshwater. The salmon swim thousands of miles. They are hunted by many **predators**. They have the race of their life to get back to their beginning. Finally they reach the place they were born. They return there to **spawn**, or lay their eggs. New life begins.

A salmon's body changes during its lifetime. Salmon are **anadromous** fish. That means they are born in freshwater. Then their bodies change. They can live in salt water. Changes happen again when they return to freshwater.

The salmon's lifetime journey is their migration. This is when an animal moves from one **habitat** to another. Migrations happen for many reasons. Some animals move to be in warmer weather where there is more food. There they can reproduce, or have their babies. And these migrations can be short distances, such as from a mountaintop to its valley. Or they can be long distances, like the salmon's journey.

There are five kinds of Pacific salmon. They are chum, sockeye, chinook, coho, and pink. Pacific salmon die after they spawn.

MIGRATION MAP

Wild salmon live in cold water in the northern third of the world. Wild Pacific salmon migrate from streams and rivers. The rivers flow into the Pacific Ocean. Pacific salmon live along the west coast of North America. They also live near Siberia and Japan. The salmon enter the Pacific Ocean. After six months to seven years, the salmon migrate back to the place they were born. Salmon have a **reproductive** migration. The length of time it takes to migrate depends on the type of wild Pacific salmon. Chinook salmon travel the farthest and stay in the ocean longest. Pink salmon travel the shortest distance. They stay in the ocean the least amount of time.

Wild Atlantic salmon migrate from streams and rivers along the east coast of North America. They also migrate from streams and rivers in northern Europe. They enter the Atlantic Ocean. After two or three years, the salmon migrate back to where they were born.

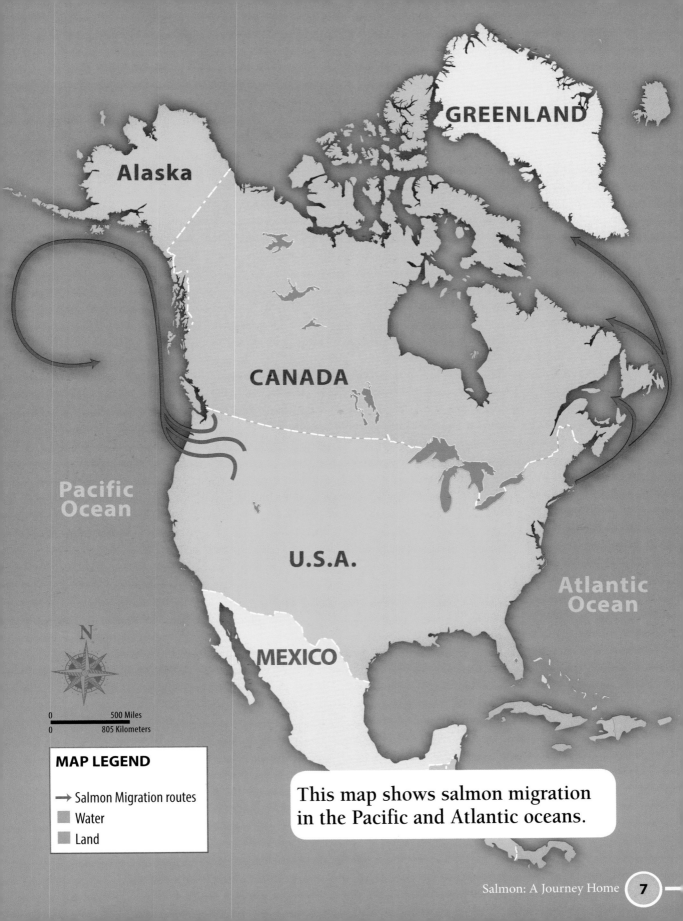

GREENLAND

Alaska

CANADA

U.S.A.

MEXICO

Pacific
Ocean

Atlantic
Ocean

N

| 0 | 500 Miles |
| 0 | 805 Kilometers |

MAP LEGEND

→ Salmon Migration routes
■ Water
■ Land

This map shows salmon migration
in the Pacific and Atlantic oceans.

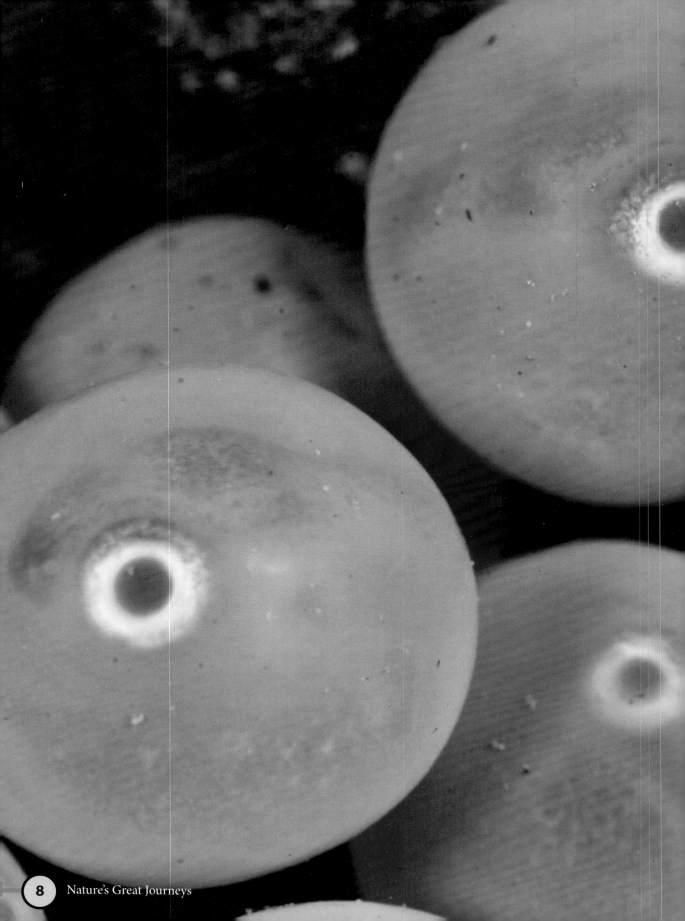

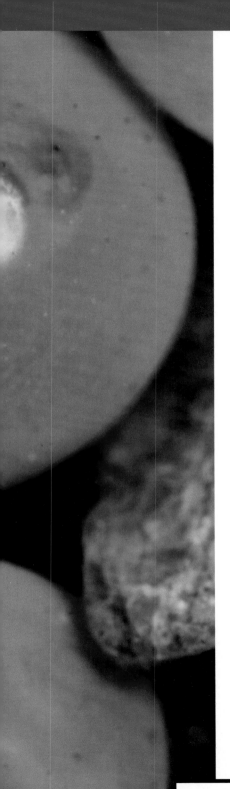

LAYING EGGS

A female reaches the stream where she was born. She is ready to lay her eggs. Once she leaves the ocean she does not eat. It takes weeks for her to return. Many females die or are eaten by predators along the way. The female is in bad shape. The long, hard trip has been tiring. She has used up most of her body fat. The salmon is holding thousands of eggs. She looks for the perfect place to lay her eggs. If more than one female wants the same place, they fight. The stronger fish wins.

The female prepares a nest with her last bit of strength. The nest is called a redd. She swishes her fins and tail to stir up gravel at the bottom of the stream. The salmon bends her body into a U shape and clears a place in the gravel. When her nest is ready, she settles into it. There she lays her eggs, or roe. The roe are round. They are pink to orange in color.

Male salmon also make the long, hard journey from the ocean to the stream. The male swims close to the female. If another male is nearby they will fight. The stronger male wins. After the female lays the roe, the male moves over them. He drops sperm, or milt, over the roe. Then the female swishes her tail back and forth. She covers the roe with gravel.

Female salmon lay their eggs, called roe, in the sandy bottom of a stream.

New salmon hatch from the eggs.

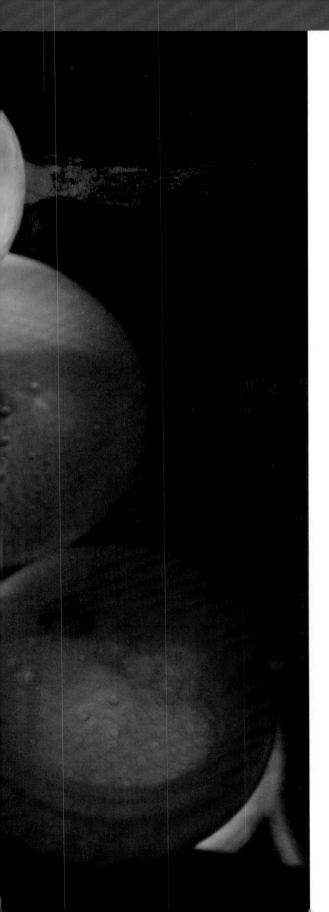

The salmon swim off. Pacific salmon never eat again. In a few days they die. Their bodies rot in the water. They add **nutrients** to the stream. They have laid their eggs in the same freshwater stream where their mothers laid their eggs. Atlantic salmon might return to the ocean. Or they might die. Atlantic salmon can spawn a few times before they die.

The roe sit in cold streams for several months. Small fish, birds, otter, and mink eat some of the roe. Others are harmed by **fungi**. But many survive. When the water warms to just the right temperature. The salmon roe begin to **hatch**.

The alevin can live up to 60 days on the food in its yolk sac.

NEW SALMON

When it hatches, the salmon is an alevin. The yolk sac of its egg is still attached to its belly. The yolk sac is the alevin's first food. The alevin begins to grow. It stays in the gravel for a few weeks. Water insects and small fish eat some of the alevin.

These young fish grow bigger and stronger. They become fry. A fry swims up into the stream. But it can still hide in the gravel for safety. It eats **plankton** and other tiny animals. The fry stay in groups for safety. Birds, snakes, insects, and other fish eat some of the fry.

When the fry grows to about 3 inches (8 cm) long, it becomes a parr. Parr marks begin to appear. Parr marks are stripes and spots on a salmon's body. The marks help the salmon blend in with its background. The parr marks are a fry's **camouflage**.

New salmon hatch from the eggs.

Pink and chum salmon reach the ocean at a younger age. Chinook, coho, sockeye, and Atlantic salmon take longer. Pink and chum salmon also return to their birth stream more quickly. Chinook take the longest time.

INTO THE SALTY OCEAN

The young salmon grow as they travel through the stream. They follow the current. The salmon tumble over waterfalls. They go through **rapids**. The salmon eat water insects and small fish. The stream becomes wider. It is now a river. The salmon move closer to the ocean.

The salmon become weaker as they travel down the river. Salmon need fresh flowing water to stay healthy. Fewer trees shade the river near the ocean. Water quality grows worse. Other fish compete for the same food.

The freshwater river meets the salty ocean in an **estuary**. Young salmon stay in the estuary for a while. That's where the salmon's body changes. The pattern on its skin changes. The stripes and spots of its parr marks fade. It becomes mostly blue-green on top. The under part of its body becomes silver. This helps keep the salmon safe in open water. In deep water, a salmon is hard to see from above. From below, its color matches the light water and sky above. Most salmon have these colors in the ocean.

A salmon goes through seven stages in its life cycle. They are egg, alevin, fry, parr, smolt, adult, and spawner.

A salmon's gills and kidneys change, too. The salmon's body needs to keep salt in its body in the ocean. In freshwater the salmon's body needs to remove salt. After these changes, the salmon becomes a smolt. It moves into the salty ocean.

Salmon face many dangers in the ocean. They are **prey** to larger fish. They are also prey to seals, sea lions, dolphins, and whales. And they are prey to people. Salmon swim in a large school. This keeps them safe. A tight school of fish might look like one big animal to a predator. Also, it is much safer to be part of a group. It is harder for a predator to pick one fish from a group.

The salmon spend several years in the ocean. Most spend two to four years at sea. Chinook salmon live in the ocean for up to six years. Wild salmon travel as far as 3,500 thousand miles (5,600 km) in their lifetime. Chum and pink salmon tend to stay near shore. Wild salmon then return to the estuary they came from. This is where they begin their long journey upstream.

Salmon bodies change so they can live in salt water.

A sockeye salmon goes back to the river after its time in the ocean.

How do the salmon know when to go home? How do they know where to go? The ocean is huge. It seems impossible that salmon can find their way home. Some scientists think salmon use the sun or stars. Others think that salmon have a sort of compass in their bodies. It may point them in the right direction. Salmon might feel ocean temperatures. The temperatures may lead them to the estuary. Some scientists think that schools of fish might remember the way. Other scientists think that salmon follow a food trail. They remember what they ate. The salmon follow the food back to the estuary.

Salmon find their way to the right estuary at the right time. But how do they know which stream to swim up? Each stream has its own smell. A salmon can smell its birth stream. Its sense of smell guides the salmon. The stream's smell leads the salmon from the coast to the spot where it was born.

THE JOURNEY UPSTREAM

Salmon leave the ocean to make a difficult upstream journey home. The rivers and streams have a current. The current flows in one direction— toward the ocean. Salmon have to swim against this current to get back to the stream. The water pushes them back. The streams go high into the hills and mountains. The salmon avoid fishing nets. If there is a dam on a river, they might swim through a fish ladder. A fish ladder is built by people. It helps migrating fish go over or through a dam. The fish leap up several levels on the fish ladder.

On their way home, the salmon leap up waterfalls. They have to make their way over rocks. Water pushes them back in rapids. In the rapids, the water moves fast. At the top of the waterfall, the salmon have to keep swimming. Or they will get pushed by water. Some salmon fall back down the waterfall or through the rapids. Then they have to begin again.

On the way upstream, salmon jump waterfalls and fight the current.

Large salmon are easy targets for predators. Predators include eagles, otters, minks, and bears. People are predators, too. Bald eagles mostly eat fish. People used to watch eagles to tell where the salmon were. Bald eagles also eat salmon that have spawned and are dead or dying. Grizzly and black bears come out of **hibernation** during the salmon's upstream journey. They mostly eat berries and other vegetable matter. But, salmon are easy food for these hungry bears.

The salmon finally arrives in the stream. It has worked very hard to return. It is thin and bony. The females' stomachs look big, though. They carry several thousand eggs.

The salmon have come so far to make sure new salmon will be born. When the redds are safely hidden, the salmon swim off upstream. Most kinds of salmon live a few days longer. Then they die. Soon a new group of salmon hatch. They begin their own journeys.

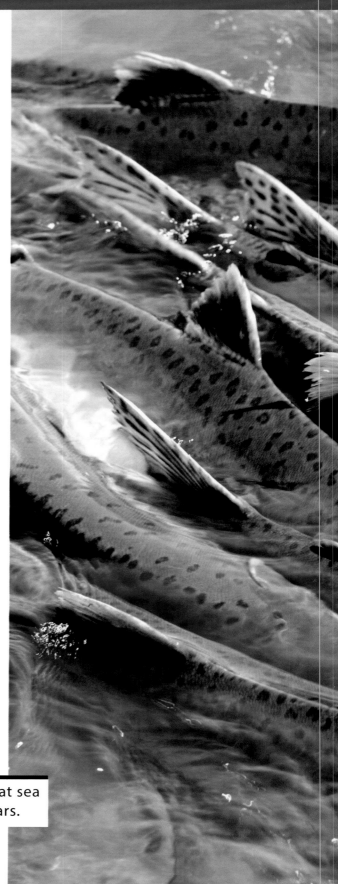

Salmon live at sea for many years.

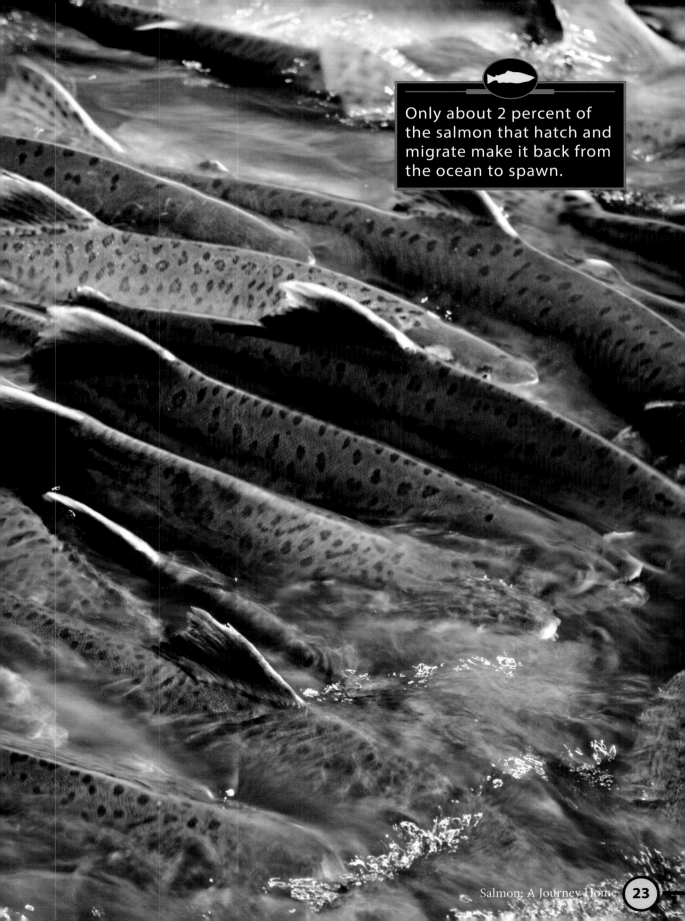

Only about 2 percent of the salmon that hatch and migrate make it back from the ocean to spawn.

THREATS TO THE SALMON

There were once many more wild salmon than there are today. Wild Atlantic salmon began to disappear long before Pacific salmon did. People came from Europe to the Atlantic coast of North America. They began to ruin the rivers. They cut down trees. They built dams. They polluted the water. They used the water to grow farm crops. They caught too many salmon.

Settlers moved from across North America. In the west, they found Pacific salmon. They began to harm the rivers of the West in the same ways. They built factories called canneries. The canneries were used to put salmon into cans. The cans of salmon could then be shipped to other places.

Canneries have stopped salmon from migrating.

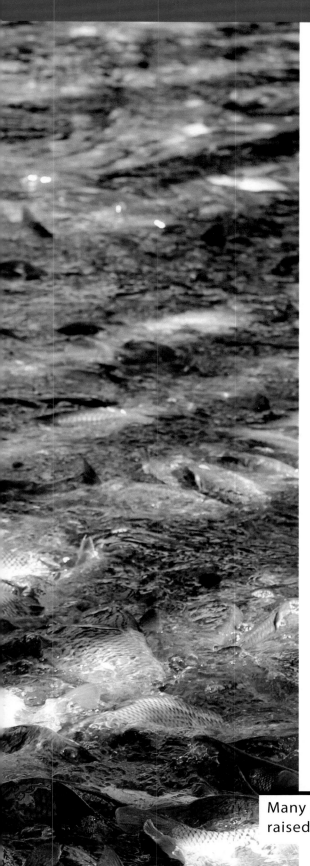

Some wild Atlantic salmon may become **extinct**. Many of the wild Pacific salmon may also become extinct. Some freshwater habitat is gone because of the changes to rivers. With loss of habitat, the salmon die. Also, it is easy to fish for salmon when they spawn.

Today, salmon farms are big businesses. Most of the salmon in stores and restaurants have been raised on farms. Many Atlantic salmon are raised in fish farms. These farms are made of huge nets or cages in the ocean. Only a small number of Atlantic salmon migrate. Salmon are raised on fish farms all over the world. They are raised in places that never had salmon before.

Raising salmon on farms causes problems. The fish live and grow in the cages. They do not migrate. They do not have much room to swim. It is easy for the salmon to get sick. The salmon can pass their illnesses to other fish. Wild salmon migrate near the cages. The wild salmon can get sick, too.

Many salmon are raised in fish farms.

With help, salmon can continue to migrate and spawn in the rivers where they were born.

People are working on ways to help the wild salmon. There are salmon **hatcheries**. These are places made by people where salmon hatch from their eggs. They stay in hatcheries for part of their lives. Then the young salmon are let go into the wild. The young salmon can then migrate. Laws limit how many wild salmon can be caught. This helps stop salmon from being over fished. And fish ladders help salmon avoid dams on rivers. With this help, wild salmon can spawn each year. They will continue their migration in Earth's oceans, rivers, and streams.

Raising fish on farms or in hatcheries is called aquaculture.

QUIZ

1 How many kinds of salmon are there?

A. Five

2 Which type of salmon spends the longest time in the ocean?

A. Chinook

3 What is an estuary?

A. Where the freshwater river meets the salty ocean

4 How many stages does the salmon life cycle have?

A. Seven

5 What percentage of the salmon that hatch and migrate make it back from the ocean to spawn?

A. About 2 percent

6 What predators do salmon face in the ocean?

A. Seals, sea lions, dolphins, whales, larger fish, people

7 When does a fry become a parr?

A. When it grows to about 3 inches (8 cm) long

8 What does a fish ladder do?

A. Helps salmon get across a dam

9 What is raising fish on farms or in hatcheries called?

A. Aquaculture

10 For how long do Chinook salmon live in the ocean?

A. Up to six years

KEY WORDS

anadromous: An anadromous fish returns from the sea to the river or stream where it was born to breed. Salmon are anadromous fish.

camouflage: Camouflage is the coloring and markings that allow an animal to blend in with its surroundings. Parr marks give young salmon camouflage.

estuary: An estuary is where freshwater and salt water mix at the wide part of a river that meets the ocean. Salmon's bodies change in an estuary.

extinct: A type of animal is extinct if it has died out. Changes to habitat may cause some salmon to become extinct.

fungi: Fungi are types of plants that have no leaves, flowers, or roots. Fungi can harm salmon roe.

habitat: A habitat is a place that has the food, water, and shelter an animal needs to survive. A salmon's habitat changes from freshwater to salt water.

hatch: To hatch is to break out of an egg. Salmon hatch in spring.

hatcheries: Hatcheries are places where eggs are hatched. Hatcheries raise young salmon and then let them go into the wild.

hibernation: Hibernation is when animals spend winters in a deep sleep. Bears wake from their hibernation and eat salmon.

nutrients: Nutrients are things that people, animals, and plants need to stay alive. Dead salmon add nutrients to a stream.

plankton: Plankton are tiny animals and plants that drift in oceans and lakes. Salmon eat plankton.

predators: Predators are animals that hunt and eat other animals. Bears are predators of salmon.

prey: Prey is an animal that is hunted for food by another animal. Salmon are the prey of humans.

rapids: Rapids are a place in a river where the water flows very quickly. Salmon swim as they migrate.

reproductive: Reproductive is something related to having babies. Salmon have a reproductive migration.

spawn: To spawn is to produce a large number of eggs. Salmon spawn in the streams where they were born.

INDEX

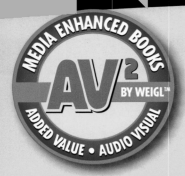

Log on to www.av2books.com

AV² by Weigl brings you media enhanced books that support active learning. Go to www.av2books.com, and enter the special code found on page 2 of this book. You will gain access to enriched and enhanced content that supplements and complements this book. Content includes video, audio, weblinks, quizzes, a slide show, and activities.

AV² Online Navigation

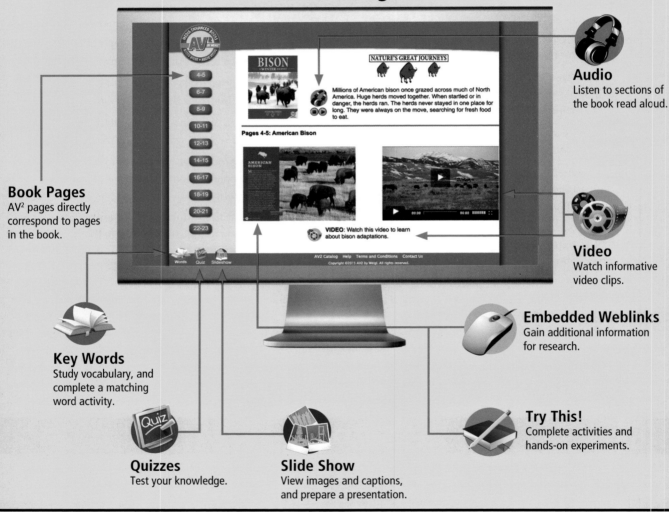

Audio
Listen to sections of the book read aloud.

Video
Watch informative video clips.

Embedded Weblinks
Gain additional information for research.

Try This!
Complete activities and hands-on experiments.

Book Pages
AV² pages directly correspond to pages in the book.

Key Words
Study vocabulary, and complete a matching word activity.

Quizzes
Test your knowledge.

Slide Show
View images and captions, and prepare a presentation.

AV² was built to bridge the gap between print and digital. We encourage you to tell us what you like and what you want to see in the future.

Sign up to be an AV² Ambassador at www.av2books.com/ambassador.